Who Is
Ketanji Brown
Jackson?

Who Is Ketanji Brown Jackson?

by Shelia P. Moses

illustrated by Dede Putra

Penguin Workshop

For my big sister, Scarlett Moses Spivey—SPM

PENGUIN WORKSHOP
An imprint of Penguin Random House LLC, New York

First published in the United States of America by Penguin Workshop,
an imprint of Penguin Random House LLC, New York, 2022

Visit us online at penguinrandomhouse.com.

Library of Congress Cataloging-in-Publication Data is available.

Printed in the United States of America

ISBN 9780593659557 (paperback)   10 9 8 7 6 5 4 3 2 1 WOR
ISBN 9780593659564 (library binding)   10 9 8 7 6 5 4 3 2 1 WOR

The publisher does not have any control over and does not assume any responsibility
for author or third-party websites or their content.

Contents

Who Is Ketanji Brown Jackson?

April 7, 2022, was no ordinary day for Judge Ketanji Brown Jackson. She was in the White House, on her way to meet with the president of the United States, to learn if she would become a Supreme Court justice. The Supreme Court is the highest court in America. It decides whether new laws agree with the United States Constitution, which is the most important set of rules in the country. The Supreme Court's decisions affect the lives of millions of people. In the more than two hundred years since the Supreme Court was established, most of the justices had been white men. And only two Black men had been appointed justices. As Ketanji walked through the halls, she hoped she would become the first Black woman to take on this important position.

Inside the Roosevelt Room, Ketanji and President Joe Biden stood next to each other as they watched Vice President Kamala Harris, the first woman and first Black person to serve in the role, on the television screen. She was leading the confirmation hearings at the United States Capitol building and was almost finished reading the votes that would decide Ketanji's future.

After going through the votes, Vice President Harris said, "On this vote, the yeas are fifty-three, the nays are forty-seven. And this nomination is confirmed." In that moment, history was made! Back in the Roosevelt Room, Ketanji and President Biden turned and hugged each other. There was no audio recording of what they said in that room, but a picture that was shared on social media showed how proud and excited Ketanji was.

Ketanji's dreams of becoming a judge one

day had brought her to the highest court in the land. After her swearing-in ceremony, which would take place in a few months, she would officially become Supreme Court Justice Ketanji Brown Jackson.

CHAPTER 1
Sunshine State

Ketanji Onyika Brown was born on September 14, 1970, in Washington, DC. Her name was suggested to her parents by her aunt, who was living in West Africa. Ketanji means "lovely one" in the Swahili language. Ketanji's parents, Johnny and Ellery, who were both raised in Miami, Florida, wanted to become educators, so they moved to Washington, DC, in the late 1960s to attend college. Like many cities in the United States at the time, Washington, DC, was the site of a large number of protests held by Black people fighting for equality. Black people were being treated terribly by many white people simply because of the color of their skin. There were laws in place that made sure Black and white people were segregated (separated). The protests increased across the country after Dr. Martin Luther King Jr., a reverend and leader who fought for equal rights, was killed in 1968. But it wasn't until the end of the 1960s that the unfair laws were removed. Buildings in Washington, DC, were damaged during these protests, but the young couple decided to stay in the nation's capital after they graduated so they could teach at public schools there.

In 1974, when Ketanji was four years old, the Brown family moved back to Florida so that Johnny could attend law school at the University of Miami. They also wanted to live closer to their families. They quickly settled into their apartment on campus. Ellery worked as a science teacher to support the family during her husband's days at law school. Years later, she became a principal at New World School of the Arts.

Since both of Ketanji's parents were educators, they taught her at an early age that school and learning were very important. By the mid-1970s, Ketanji had entered preschool and developed a love for reading. She spent her evenings at the kitchen table with her father and his stack of law schoolbooks. She colored in her coloring books while her daddy studied hard. As the years

passed, she got her own set of schoolbooks and studied along with him. While Ketanji was still in elementary school, Johnny passed the bar and became a lawyer for the Miami-Dade County School Board. The whole family was very proud of him, especially Ketanji.

When Ketanji was ten years old, her baby brother, Ketajh, was born. Although there was a big age difference, she enjoyed being his big sister and spending time with him and their parents. The Browns needed more space, so they moved out of their apartment and into a house in the suburbs of Miami. The family filled their home with love, laughter, and, of course, books for the children. Even though Ketanji and her family lived in a majority white neighborhood, their neighbors were nice, and Ketanji became friends with many of the kids.

Ketajh and Ketanji both did very well in school. In junior high school, Ketanji joined the debate team and soon her teachers realized that she was a great public speaker. A debate is a competition where people make arguments for or against a topic, and judges decide whose argument is the best. Ketanji often won the debates she competed in, and so she joined the debate team when she went to Miami

Palmetto Senior High School. Her debate coach, Fran Berger, was very committed to her students. She got up early to meet them before the school bell rang each morning so that they could practice. She and the debate team sometimes stayed after school and met on weekends to prepare for competitions. Ketanji was so good on the debate team that she won the 1988 national oratory title at the National Catholic Forensic League in New Orleans, Louisiana, when she was in the twelfth grade.

When Ketanji flew with her debate team to a competition at Harvard University in Cambridge, Massachusetts, she fell in love with the campus after just one visit. She later told her parents she wanted to attend Harvard after graduation. She also knew what she wanted to study at Harvard. She wanted to be a lawyer just like her father!

Making good grades and winning debates were not the only interests Ketanji had. She loved acting and participated in school plays, but it was not always easy for Ketanji to get speaking roles at a school that was 73 percent white. In her senior year, Ketanji was very upset when her drama teacher told her she could not be considered for a part in a school play about a white family because she was Black. And her school counselor even tried to discourage Ketanji from following her dream of attending Harvard. "Don't set your sights so high," the counselor told her. But Ketanji's parents told her she could do anything and be whatever she wanted to be, so she continued to set her sights high.

Ketanji became secretary of the National Honor Society at her high school, was elected class president three times, and was inducted into her school's hall of fame. In her senior yearbook she wrote, "I want to go into law and eventually have a judicial appointment." Ketanji's classmates voted her "most likely to succeed." And she graduated with honors in 1988.

CHAPTER 2
College Years

In the fall of 1988, Ketanji began attending Harvard University. Being fifteen hundred miles away from her family was hard for her, but she knew that going to Harvard was an important opportunity. Ketanji became fast friends with her roommates, Antoinette, Nina, and Lisa, who were very kind. But no matter how much they had in common or how much fun they had together, she still missed her family. She had been on campus only a few weeks when she found herself sitting on the steps outside the library crying. No one knew it was her birthday. When she finally returned to her dorm room, she turned on her answering machine and saw her mother had left her a message. Ellery was singing to her daughter for her birthday, and the beautiful sound of her mother's voice made Ketanji feel so much better.

As time passed, Ketanji got involved in student activities and joined the Black Students Association at her school. Even after making new friends, though, there were problems ahead that the young freshman didn't see coming.

While on campus, Ketanji noticed a Confederate battle flag hanging from one of the white student's dorm room window. This flag was used during the Civil War by Southern states that supported the institution of slavery. Many people of color, especially Black people, see this flag as a symbol of hatred. The Black students read the message loud and clear. They weren't welcomed by everyone at Harvard.

After attending a meeting with other members of the Black Students Association, Ketanji and the group decided to stage a protest demanding that the school administration ask the student to remove the offensive flag. But while the members were out protesting, they were missing classes and study time. In one of the meetings, Ketanji spoke out. "Wait a minute, as we're doing this, we're missing out on classes. As we're fighting against this injustice, we're actually doing them a service because we're going to be failing," she said. After that day, the students continued to protest but they did so in between and after classes to make sure that they never missed another class. A few weeks later, the university administration said the student was allowed to display his flag in the window. Even though this wasn't the answer Ketanji was hoping for, she was glad she spoke up.

No matter how many obstacles got in her way, Ketanji was determined to do well at Harvard and enjoy her college years. She enrolled in several drama classes. Matt Damon, who later became an award-winning actor, was her scene partner in one of her drama courses. To improve her acting skills, she joined an

improvisational group called On Thin Ice. Improvisation is a type of acting where most or all of what is performed is unscripted and created on the spot. Ketanji also joined a production

Ketanji and members of On Thin Ice

group called Black C.A.S.T., which developed Black theater productions on campus.

No matter what was happening at school, her parents were always a phone call away. They often made the long journey to Cambridge to visit their daughter.

During her junior year, she found herself protesting again. The students noticed there weren't enough full-time faculty members in the school's African American Studies Department. Ketanji and a large group of Black students wore black clothing to the football games instead of crimson and white (the school's colors). They wanted to get the alumni's attention. Many students of other races supported the Black students in their fight for justice on and off campus. One of the white students she met in college was Boston native Patrick Jackson, whom she met when she was a sophomore. They eventually began dating and fell in love.

In 1992, Ketanji graduated with the high honor of magna cum laude with a bachelor of arts degree. She moved to New York for her first job, as a writer and researcher for *Time* magazine. She wrote stories about prescription drug prices and economic policies. She worked at this job for a year before entering Harvard's school of law in the fall of 1993.

She was an excellent law school student, and she became a supervising editor of the *Harvard Law Review.* She took her studies and responsibilities very seriously. In 1996, Ketanji graduated from Harvard Law School with honors, reaching one of the big goals she had set for herself when she was still in high school.

CHAPTER 3
The Lawyer and Courtroom Clerk

Her graduation in 1996 wasn't the only event Ketanji celebrated that year. With her family and friends there to celebrate with them, she and Patrick got married. He had graduated from Harvard and went on to attend Columbia University's medical school in New York. After graduating from Columbia in 1995, he moved back to Cambridge and worked as a surgical resident at Massachusetts General Hospital.

One of Ketanji's classmates also got married that year, so she flew to Chicago to attend the wedding. Ketanji recognized one of the guests and asked her friend to make an introduction. She was thrilled to meet Harvard Law School alumnus Barack Obama, an attorney who had

also been the first Black president of the *Harvard Law Review*. Filled with excitement, she asked another friend to snap their picture.

After the wedding, Ketanji returned to

Ketanji meets Barack Obama

Cambridge and settled into her life as a newlywed. She landed a job as a law clerk for Judge Patti B. Saris at the Massachusetts District Court for a year. She spent long hours drafting the judge's orders and opinions and assisted Judge Saris during courtroom proceedings. Patrick was still a surgical resident at Massachusetts General Hospital, where he sometimes worked twenty-four-hour shifts. But even after long hours at the hospital, Patrick would rush across town to watch and support his wife in the courtroom.

The next year, Ketanji applied for a position as a clerk for Judge Bruce M. Selya of the US Court of Appeals for the First Circuit. She knew that taking the position meant moving to Rhode Island and being away from her husband, but she had Patrick's full support. Ketanji told Judge Selya, "If you make me an offer, I will accept it and I will move to Providence." That is exactly what the ambitious young lawyer did. This decision was difficult for the couple, but they knew it was the right choice for her career.

Between 1998 and 2002, Ketanji would take several positions, including working at private law firms. She also clerked for Supreme Court Justice Stephen Breyer in 1999. Her work eventually brought Ketanji back to Massachusetts. In 2000, Ketanji went back to working at a law firm and gave birth to her and Patrick's first daughter, Talia. The young couple was excited about their new healthy baby, but they were unhappy about being away from her so much. They both worked long hours at the hospital and the law firm. Even though the firm fully supported her, Ketanji knew she had to make a change for the sake of her family.

CHAPTER 4
A Dream Come True

In 2002, Ketanji and Patrick decided to move their family to Washington, DC, where Patrick would take a position as a doctor at MedStar Georgetown University Hospital. Ketanji worked at a private practice firm for a year, then joined the US Sentencing Commission as an assistant special counsel. The Sentencing Commission is an organization in the judicial branch of the government that develops federal sentencing policy. That means they get to make rules about how to punish people and organizations that commit crimes against the country. Though Ketanji and Patrick were still busy, they would have time to spend with Talia after work.

The family of three adjusted to their new life

in Washington, DC, and they were overjoyed when their second daughter, Leila, was born in 2004. Ketanji was also happy to be living near her little brother who stayed in the DC area after graduating from Howard University. Ketajh was an officer for the Baltimore Police Department.

He also joined the Maryland National Guard. Johnny and Ellery were very proud of their son and daughter. They were still living in Miami and came to visit their children often.

In 2005, Ketanji decided to make another career change. She became a federal public

defender. Federal public defenders are attorneys who handle criminal trials in the US federal court system. They provide legal advice and support for accused criminals who do not have money to pay for a lawyer.

Her position as a federal public defender brought Ketanji attention from national newspapers and television news shows. In some of her cases, she represented people who were imprisoned by the United States in Guantanamo Bay, Cuba. The people held at Guantanamo Bay were considered potential war criminals. Many lawyers would not defend prisoners of war, but Ketanji made sure they were given a fair trial. Her new position meant she was also able to fight for racial justice for some of her clients. This meant a lot to Ketanji, just as it did in college when she saw the Confederate flag hanging in the white student's window at Harvard.

Ketanji left the District of Columbia's public

defender's office in 2007. She was not interested in becoming a politician but was very happy that Barack Obama, whom she had met in 1996, was now a US senator and a candidate for president of the United States of America. She became a poll monitor for his campaign. Like many Americans, Ketanji celebrated when Obama was elected as the forty-fourth president of the United States in 2008.

In 2009, President Obama nominated Ketanji to serve as a member of the US Sentencing Commission after hearing about her accomplishments from the White House research team. She waited nervously for confirmation. As usual, she turned to her mother for comfort. Ellery had introduced Ketanji to crochet, a type of needlework that uses thread or yarn to make clothes and other items, when she was a child. Now, Ketanji picked up a book on crochet and learned how to make hats and scarves.

She also taught herself how to knit, which she still does today. Ketanji was confirmed by the Senate in 2010 and became vice chair of the commission. In 2012, Obama nominated her to be a judge for the US District Court for the

District of Columbia, but the Senate didn't hold a vote. President Obama nominated her again in 2013. This time she was confirmed. In May 2013, she was sworn in by Justice Breyer, for whom she had clerked as a young lawyer.

Ketanji Brown Jackson is sworn in as a district judge by Justice Stephen Breyer

She proudly settled into her new office and hung the picture of her with Barack Obama in 1996 on the wall.

Ketanji was a judge now, just as she dreamed when she was in high school. And even though her workdays were long, she decided that her main job was being a mother, so she juggled her daughters' busy schedules and made sure they ate dinner together as a family. Her girls understood the importance of their mother's work.

After Justice Antonin Scalia died in 2016, Ketanji's daughter Leila, then eleven years old, came home from school and told her mother she should apply for the job. She explained to Leila that the US president nominates a Supreme Court justice. After listening to her mother, Leila went to her room and wrote a letter to President Obama to suggest he nominate her mother. She wrote: "Dear Mr. President, while you are considering judges to fill Justice Scalia's seat on the Supreme Court, I would like to add my mother, Ketanji Brown Jackson, of the district court to the list." She went on to relay that her mother was "an excellent fit for the position."

Although Ketanji wasn't nominated then, she wasn't discouraged.

The Federal Court System

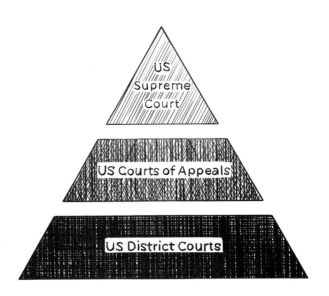

There are three levels of the federal court system in the United States. The lowest level is made up of the US District Courts. They cover different regions of the country and handle most federal cases. The second level holds the Courts of Appeals. They review cases of those who believe their case wasn't handled fairly. At the top of the system is the Supreme Court, which has the final say. All federal and Supreme Court judges are appointed by the president of the United States and must be confirmed by the US Senate before they can begin working in these courts. Federal judges are able to keep these jobs for the rest of their lives.

CHAPTER 5
The Highest Court

In 2020, people were getting ready to vote for the next president of the United States of America. One of the candidates, Democrat Joe Biden, made a promise that if he were elected, he would appoint the first Black woman to the Supreme Court. For over four hundred years, Black people in America have been mistreated and overlooked. Even though some things have improved, the Supreme Court justices had stayed largely white and male.

After Joe Biden won the election, people began to discuss whom he would nominate if a seat on the Supreme Court became available. Ketanji had President Biden's attention, and since no Supreme Court seats were vacant, he nominated her to become a judge on the US Court of Appeals for the DC Circuit in 2021. Most Republican senators did not support Ketanji's nomination, but she went on to be confirmed to the US Court of Appeals on June 14, 2021. That same year, she received Columbia University Law School's Constance Baker Motley Award for giving back to the community, advancing the rights of people, and empowering women of color.

In late January 2022, Supreme Court Justice Stephen Breyer formally announced his retirement after serving for twenty-seven years. The question many in the news media asked was, who would replace Justice Breyer? Names of Black judges were brought up, including Ketanji's.

On February 25, 2022, President Biden kept his promise, and nominated Ketanji Brown Jackson to become the 116th associate justice of the US Supreme Court. News reports across the country mentioned that if she was confirmed, Ketanji would become the first justice in US history who had been a federal public defender and clerked for three federal judges. The people who had earlier opposed Ketanji's confirmation to the US Court of Appeals were also set against her becoming a judge on the Supreme Court. Regardless of the opposition, the Senate Judiciary Committee approved her nomination, and her confirmation hearing was set to begin in March.

On March 24, 2022, on the fourth day of the confirmation hearing, Ketanji sat in front of a panel of twenty-two Senate Judiciary Committee members in the Capitol building in Washington, DC. They asked her questions about her career and the decisions she had made as a lawyer and judge. The Democratic senators on the Judiciary Committee were in favor of Ketanji's nomination, but most of the Republicans were not, and they asked harsh questions during the hearing.

Ketanji remained strong as her family and friends gathered around her. Her daughters sat beside their father and smiled even during the difficult moments of their mother's confirmation hearing. Back in Miami, the teachers at her former high school allowed some students to watch the confirmation hearing on television. They were so proud, especially the debate team.

During her opening statements, Ketanji had special words for her daughters, Leila and Talia. She said, "Girls, I know it has not been easy as I have tried to navigate the challenges of juggling my career and motherhood. . . . But I hope you have seen that with hard work, determination, and love, it can be done."

She also talked about her hard work as a federal judge. "I have been a judge for nearly a decade now, and I take that responsibility and my duty to be independent very seriously." Step by step, she explained her journey and closed by saying,

"Thank you for this historic chance to join the highest Court, to work with brilliant colleagues, to inspire future generations, and to ensure liberty and justice for all."

On April 7, 2022, the senators began to cast their votes while Vice President Kamala Harris listened. Three of the favorable votes were from Republicans Susan Collins, Mitt Romney, and Lisa Murkowski, who believed Ketanji would make a great Supreme Court justice.

Vice President Harris beamed with joy when she announced the fifty-three to forty-seven vote in Ketanji's favor. She was a couple miles away at the White House with President Biden watching the votes being announced on national television. It was official! She had now become the first Black woman to sit on the Supreme Court. President Biden turned and gave Ketanji a hug and the moment was captured in a picture.

The following day, Ketanji gave a brief speech at the White House celebration on the front lawn. She thanked the American people, President Biden, her teachers, friends, family, and her ancestors. She ended by saying, "I have now achieved something far beyond anything my grandparents could've possibly ever imagined. But no one does this on their own . . . in the poetic words of Dr. Maya Angelou, I do so now, while 'bringing the gifts . . . my ancestors gave. I am the dream and the hope of the slave.'"

On June 30, 2022, the Jackson family arrived at the Supreme Court building for Ketanji's swearing-in ceremony. As Chief Justice John Roberts administered the Constitutional Oath and retired justice Stephen Breyer administered the Judicial Oath, Ketanji stood by Patrick, who was holding the family bible and a bible donated by Justice John Marshall Harlan. Their daughters, and many television viewers at home, watched

Ketanji Brown Jackson become the first Black woman justice in the highest court in the land.

Timeline of
Ketanji Brown Jackson's Life

1970 — Ketanji Onyika Brown is born in Washington, DC

1974 — Moves to Miami, Florida

1988 — Graduates from Miami Palmetto Senior High School

1992 — Graduates from Harvard University

1993 — Moves to New York and works for *Time* magazine

1994 — Returns to Cambridge, Massachusetts, to attend Harvard Law School

1996 — Graduates cum laude from Harvard Law School and marries Patrick Graves Jackson

1999 — Serves as clerk on the Supreme Court for Justice Breyer

2000 — Daughter Talia is born

2003 — Becomes an assistant special counsel for the US Sentencing Commission

2004 — Daughter Leila is born

2005 — Becomes a federal public defender in Washington, DC

2010 — Serves as vice chair of US Sentencing Commission

2013 — Becomes a judge for the US District Court for the District of Columbia

2021 — Serves on the US Court of Appeals for the DC Circuit

2022 — Nominated to the Supreme Court

— Confirmed on April 7 and sworn in on June 30

Timeline of the World

1972 — Shirley Chisholm, the first Black woman to be elected to the US Congress, runs for president of the United States

1982 — Constance Baker Motley, the first Black female federal judge in America, is appointed chief justice of the US District Court for the Southern District of New York

1990 — South African activist and leader Nelson Mandela is freed from prison after twenty-seven years

1992 — Mae C. Jemison becomes the first Black woman in space, onboard the space shuttle *Endeavour*

2002 — Halle Berry becomes the first Black woman to win an Academy Award for best actress

2005 — Condoleezza Rice becomes the first Black female US secretary of state

2008 — Barack Obama is elected the forty-fourth president of the United States

2013 — Alicia Garza, Opal Tometi, and Patrisse Cullors start the Black Lives Matter organization

2016 — The National Museum of African American History and Culture opens in Washington, DC

2021 — President Joe Biden declares Juneteenth a federal holiday

2022 — LeBron James becomes first active NBA player in history to become a billionaire

Bibliography

Hounshell, Blake, and Leah Askarinam. "Democrats' Defense of Ketanji Brown Jackson Leaves Some Wanting More." *New York Times*, April 8, 2022.

Hulse, Carl, and Annie Karni. "Jackson Confirmed as First Black Woman to Sit on Supreme Court." *New York Times*, April 7, 2022.

Leibowitz, Aaron, Jay Weaver, and Bryan Lowry. "Supreme Court Prospect Brown Jackson Was 'Star in the Making' at Miami's Palmetto High." *Miami Herald*, January 26, 2022.

Websites

www.whitehouse.gov

www.splcenter.org

YOUR HEADQUARTERS FOR HISTORY

Activities, Mad Libs, and sidesplitting jokes!
Discover the Who HQ books beyond the biographies

.